A STUDENT'S GUIDE TO

SANCTIFICATION

LIGON DUNCAN
& JOHN PERRITT

TRACK
DOCTRINE

D1111966

A STUDENT'S GUIDE TO
SANCTIFICATION

TRACK DOCTRINE

LIGON DUNCAN & JOHN PERRITT

Scripture quotations are from *The Holy Bible, English Standard Version*, copyright © 2001 by Crossway Bibles, a publishing ministry of Good News Publishers. Used by permission. All rights reserved. ESV Text Edition: 2011.

10 9 8 7 6 5 4 3 2 1

First published in 2020
by
Christian Focus Publications Ltd,
Geanies House, Fearn, Ross-shire,
IV20 1TW, Great Britain
www.christianfocus.com

with

Reformed Youth Ministries,
1445 Rio Road East
Suite 201D
Charlottesville,
Virginia, 22911

Cover by MOOSE77

Printed by Gutenberg, Malta

CONTENTS

Series Introduction

Christianity is a religion of words, because our God is a God of words. He created through words, calls Himself the Living Word, and wrote a book (filled with words) to communicate to His children. In light of this, pastors and parents should take great efforts to train the next generation to be readers; *Track* is a series designed to do exactly that.

Written for students, the *Track* series addresses a host of topics in three primary areas: Doctrine, Culture, & the Christian Life. *Track's* books are theologically rich, yet accessible. They seek to engage and challenge the student without dumbing things down.

One definition of a track reads, *a way that has been formed by someone else's footsteps.* The goal of the *Track* series is to point us to that 'someone else' – Jesus Christ. The One who forged a track to guide His followers. While we cannot follow this track perfectly, by His grace and Spirit He calls us to strive to stay on the path. It is our prayer that this series of books would help guide Christ's Church until He returns.

In His Service,

John Perritt
RYM's Director of Resources
Series Editor

Introduction[1]

Have you ever been to a summer camp? I went when I was in second grade, but came home because I got homesick. Much later, when I was in college, I served as a camp counselor – thankfully I didn't leave early like I did in second grade. Even though I didn't have to come home, I did get a little homesick.

It wasn't a homesickness that dominated my time at camp, but I did miss certain things. One aspect of homesickness is the loss of what's familiar. The sights, sounds and smells of 'home' are removed, and we long for them.

Through this homesickness, I noticed something that summer as a camp counselor. When I was removed from my family and friends, I missed many things. One surprising

1   For the original article by Ligon Duncan, visit https://ligonduncan.com/the-good-news-of-progressive-sanctification-21-encouragements/ Last accessed November 2019.

thing I missed had to do with language. Specifically, I missed the lingo and inside jokes I could share with my friends back home. I had been taken from a familiar context to a new context where my language was foreign. Yes, we all spoke English at this camp, but the stories and one-liners I heard from others were unfamiliar to me. In a sense, I had to learn a new language with new people.

In Christianity, we have some similarities. Often times we can use 'churchy' words. Words like – justification or sanctification. Phrases like 'in Christ' or 'the finished work of Jesus'. Words and phrases that may be familiar to many of us and roll off our tongues with ease, are words and phrases that are like a foreign language to others.

This book will highlight one of those church words 'sanctification.' It can be defined as follows: *Sanctification is the work of God's free grace, whereby we are renewed in the whole man after the image of God, and are enabled more and more to die unto sin, and live unto righteousness.*[1] In short, sanctification is simply a word used to describe the life of the Christian on earth. It is a life lived in the pursuit of godliness. Christians

---

1   Westminster Shorter Catechism.

cannot attain perfection by their work and effort, but they strive to become more like Jesus by the power of the Holy Spirit.

Often Christians receive great encouragement about their justification (if they take the time to think about it). If you haven't given much thought to it, consider this. Justification says that by faith in the finished work of Jesus, you are declared perfect and righteous. Not just perfect and righteous in the opinion of various people. But perfect and righteous before the holy God of all creation – how could that not be encouraging?

To know that your sins – past, present, and future – have been paid for on the cross and that Christ's righteousness has been given to you should, at the very least, bring a smile to your face. It's an amazing truth of God's grace to sinners like you and me.

Yet while Christians are sometimes encouraged by their justification, they are more often discouraged about their sanctification (or seeming lack thereof). Christians can know and believe that they've truly been justified by the finished work of Jesus, but when they look at the same old patterns of failure, they can be moved to doubt. *Am I really a Christian? Am I really growing in grace? Do I, by grace, see any 'progress' against sin and temptation?*

Often times justification is described as a 'one-time act.' That is, God, once-and-for-all, declares Christians as 'justified' the moment they believe in Jesus. Sanctification, on the other hand, can be referred to as an 'ongoing work', where the Christian grows in grace and becomes more like Jesus. No human can become fully sinless this side of heaven, but there can be growth. A Christian can become more *sanctified*.

Talking about sanctification can make many Christians uncomfortable. They can become uncomfortable because it sounds like we're talking about perfection (which we're not). It can make people uncomfortable because it can sound like you're judging others (we're not doing that either). However, I believe this is important to talk about, which should be obvious since I'm taking the time to write this. I believe it's important for many reasons, but one is that Christians can often miss out on something that is intended to be a blessing from God.

Yes, justification should be encouraging to a Christian, but so should sanctification.

Sanctification is a blessing from God for His glory and the Christian's good. Therefore, I want to take the remainder of this short book to pass along encouragements of sanctification. I want to share with you the good news of sanctification. It's a truth that should – like justification – bring a smile to your face. It's easy to memorize a definition for sanctification, but I want you to think about how the biblical truth of sanctification will change your life.

One last thing. There will be more 'churchy' words and phrases throughout this book. Use the short glossary found on page 71 as often as needed.

1. Watch Your Mouth!

Most of us have said a bad word (or two) in our lifetime. Most of us have also gotten in trouble when we said the word that was off limits. Whether it was a parent, grandparent, teacher, or pastor, they heard the word and enforced the punishment. Truth be told, we probably deserved it.

Defining bad words can be difficult. What's bad in one culture might not be bad in another culture. That said, we know there are words we should and shouldn't use. The Bible has plenty of passages that warn us about how we use our words, and God has also given us a conscience that warns us when we're saying (or doing or thinking) something we probably shouldn't.

Well, holiness isn't a word you'd likely get in trouble for. I doubt if you screamed the word – *Sanctification!* – you'd get grounded (unless you screamed this at 1 in the morning in your parents' bedroom). While you might not get in trouble for saying 'holy' or 'sanctification,' these can sound like bad words to some Christians. At the very least, these are words loaded with controversy and debate.

SOME FANCY WORDS

There are also some bad mottos about sanctification, not to mention some bad approaches to sanctification in the church or Christian circles (perhaps because of the discouragements associated with it). Sometimes there's preaching and teaching that attempts to avoid sounding careless about sanctification, so the sermon or lesson ends up sounding like a lecture. The speaker uses so many imperatives (maybe even yells a lot) and fails to root Christian effort in God's grace.

Perhaps the passionate preacher is telling Christians to fight sin, but is not clear about God's grace that is at work in us? Maybe the teacher has not been clear to tell us that, by faith, God sees us clothed in the righteousness of Christ? If that's the case, the preaching and teaching can end up sounding like: 'Be good, do better, try harder.'

Sometimes preaching that seeks to avoid sounding too harsh ends up never challenging other Christians. In these sermons/lessons, the preacher/teacher seems to explain challenges away in a manner that makes them all sound like Christians don't have a responsibility to live a certain way.

If they come across any exhortation or imperative in the Bible, it may sound a bit like this, 'The Bible says for you to do x, but you can't do x because you are a sinner, but praise God Jesus did x for you, so stop trying to do what you can't do and rest in His grace.'

Both of these are incorrect approaches to the Bible. They are wrong and unbiblical. The person who teaches that the law doesn't matter is referred to as an '**antinomian.**' The person who teaches that you are saved by your work and effort is referred to as a '**legalist.**' Both the antinomian and the legalist are wrong.

Sinclair Ferguson explains that both the antinomian and the legalist are obsessed with the law. They both place too much emphasis on it. Even though one seems to dismiss it (antinomian) and one seems to live by it (legalist), they both look to the law in an unbiblical way. The Christian, however, is to look to Christ and see His finished work. The Christian is to work, but work in the grace God gives. Now, I'm getting ahead of myself, so just know this will all be explained in the pages ahead.

PERFORM FROM ACCEPTANCE

In Rankin Wilbourne's book, *Union with Christ*, he shares an example from the television show, *American Idol*, that I'll paraphrase. He talks about the nervousness that every contestant on the show deals with. They all battle a form of nervousness when they are performing because they have not been accepted on the show or have not been accepted to advance on the show. However, when the next *American Idol* winner is chosen, they get to perform one last time. As Wilbourne points out, this final performance is a performance from acceptance and the nerves seem to fade away.

Sanctification has many parallels to this situation. In sanctification, it's neither 'try harder' nor 'stop trying' but 'by grace, grow.' Or, to put it another way 'by grace, become who God created and redeemed you to be.' In other words, you've already been *accepted* because of the finished work of Christ; now work by His grace.

You see, the grace exhortations and imperatives of sanctification are based on really good news – you're accepted in Jesus! When you hear, 'You can't change, so stop trying' that's NOT good news. When you hear, 'You are on your own in sanctification, so just make a better effort', that's NOT good news.

Here's the good news – your justification and sanctification have the same root of God's grace. Your progress in sanctification, your growth in godliness, is just as much God's gracious work in you as is your justification. That is, His freely justifying, pardoning and accepting of you on the basis of Christ's work and the work He calls you to do is by His grace alone. And this is REALLY, REALLY good news!

Main Point

We do good works because we know that God has already accepted us through His Son.

2. The Focus of Sanctification

KEEP YOUR EYE ON THE BALL

There was a former student in my youth ministry who was very athletic. He had a lot of natural skill and talent. So much so, that many talked about him playing on the 'next level.' One thing that was interesting was a correction to his game that allowed him to do even better. What was that correction? Glasses.

This student was already doing well in football. In most games he was one of the fastest, if not the fastest, player on the field. He would catch the ball easily and make many plays. However, his father took him to get glasses, and the son was amazed. After a game or practice (I can't remember), he made a comment along these lines, *Dad, I love my new glasses. I can actually see the ball!*

This student was already performing well. He was successful on the field. But he couldn't see! Now, that's not totally true. He could see, but he could not see all that well. Things were often blurry and created challenges that hindered him from performing to the best of his ability.

In the last chapter we talked about performance in the Christian life. The Bible tells us that we cannot perform to earn God's favor. As Dallas Willard says, 'Grace is not opposed to effort. It is opposed to earning.'[1]

However, we are to work as Christians, but this work is by God's grace, and it is a work that's done with the knowledge that we are accepted because of Christ's work. In short, we work knowing Christ already worked for us.

Like the story of my student who needed glasses, the glasses of the Christian are very important. In the case of our sanctification, we need to have the proper 'biblical lenses' to view sanctification. Because of our sin, our heart and eyes will be blurred, and we will think improperly about sanctification. In this chapter, I want to give you **four truths** that should give you a proper 'vision' (or understanding) of sanctification.

---

1   Dallas Willard, 'Live Life to the Full', http://www. dwillard.org/articles/individual/live-life-to-the-full Last accessed December 2019.

GOD CARES MORE ABOUT YOUR SANCTIFICATION THAN YOU DO[2]

Preaching and teaching God's Word is a very humbling reality. Whenever you're telling someone what God's Word says, or how we should apply God's Word, it's intimidating... to say the least. It's why God's Word actually warns that teachers of the Word will be judged more harshly. One truth that always encourages me, however, is this: *God loves His Word more than I do. God cares about His church more than I do. God cares about His people in the church more than I do.* In other words, God's truth is not ultimately dependent upon me and my preaching and teaching. His truth will go forward without me.

In a related manner, God cares more about your sanctification than you do. As we've already said, sanctification has everything to do with God's grace. God's grace exceeds our proper understanding of sanctification. Sanctification has everything to do with Christ's finished work, and God loves, affirms, and was (and still is) well-pleased with His Son. Because of Jesus, God loves His children and will be sure to work alongside them as they seek to live

---

2   Philippians 2:13.

as His children. Which leads us to the second truth.

GOD IS ALWAYS WORKING ON OUR SANCTIFICATION[3]

It's funny to think about our motivation for certain prayers. Sometimes we pray for patience or pray that we won't worry or pray that we won't get angry. Even though it's good to pray about patience, worry, and anger, our motivation can be selfish. Sometimes when we pray these things, we're actually saying, *God, please take away any circumstances that would test my patience. God please keep everyone safe and happy so I'll be happy and not worry.* In short, our prayer is really, *God, make my life easy.*

However, when you pray for patience, God might answer that by giving you traffic. A slow internet connection. Difficulty in relationships. Or any number of providences that test your patience.

We know that God does not tempt us, and we know that He's not some cosmic prankster trying to pick on His children. That said, He longs for His children to be more conformed to the image of His beautiful Son. Therefore, the

---

3   Philippians 2:13.

challenges and difficulties in your life are often God's providences that are used to sanctify you throughout your daily life.

SANCTIFICATION IS FIRST AND FOREMOST GOD'S WORK

This truth is very closely related to the previous one. It is proper to say that the Bible is ultimately about God... not us. Well, sanctification is also ultimately about God... not us.

Even though sanctification is viewed as the Christian's work, by the Spirit, to become more like Jesus, the root and foundation is ultimately God. It's God's work because it has everything to do with His plan, His purpose, His promise to redeem a people, by the power of the Spirit, through the finished work of Jesus.

While justification is God's work FOR us, sanctification is God's work IN us.

SANCTIFICATION MEANS GROWTH WILL HAPPEN

Lastly, sanctification means you WILL grow. For the Christian, spiritual growth can often be discouraging. It can feel like you are always battling with the same sins. It can seem like you're always asking God to forgive you for that *one* thing. Progress seems like an impossibility, if there's even such thing as progress in the Christian life.

The reality of sanctification, however, is that you WILL progress. Because God's grace is beyond our comprehension, He is always at work. He never grows tired. He never grows weary. He never gets annoyed at forgiving people – He loves to forgive! His work of sanctification is always effective. Even though you might not feel like you're growing as a Christian, you are. God promises you will.

As we move forward in our understanding of sanctification, our focus is vital. Yes, sanctification has much to do with your growth as a child of God, but as God's child, keep your primary focus on your Father... not you.

Main Point

We need to focus on sanctification, expecting God to change us.

3. The Freedom of Sanctification

THIS IS GOING TO HURT ME...

If someone were to make a 'Top 10' list of clichéd statements parents make, *This is going to hurt me, more than it hurts you,* would probably be at the top. Sure, *Because I said so,* or *Eat your vegetables*, might be up there as well, but we've all heard some form of the first statement.

While the statement may be slightly disingenuous at times, there is some truth to it. Whenever a parent punishes a child – with whatever form they choose – it hurts the parent. No parent gets pleasure out of making their child miserable, but the parent has the 'greater good' in mind. That greater good? The ultimate well-being of their child.

When it comes to our sanctification, we can often have similar thoughts. Sanctification is often painful and seems like some sort of punishment from God. It can seem like God doesn't want us to have any fun. It can seem like He's the grumpy old-man who's stuck in the past, or like the overly-authoritative parent who isn't happy unless no one is happy.

Even though sanctification may be painful at times, it has the long view in mind. Sanctification may feel like a burden or a life filled with meaningless boundaries. Yet, because we have a loving Heavenly Father, sanctification is actually something that brings us great freedom.

THE FREEDOM OF SANCTIFICATION

The Christian life is a life of freedom. When Jesus saves us, He frees us! Therefore, in the Christian life we are and must and will be free! Think about that last sentence. The words *are, must* and *will* sound so demanding – you *are* going to do this, you *must* do that, and you *will* obey me.

However, when you think about those words through the work Jesus completed, it changes everything. In essence, Jesus is saying, *Because I bought you with my righteous life and atoning death, you are free, you must be free, and you will be free.*

You see, our sinful nature makes us think boundaries and commands are burdensome.

Thinking back to the image of the parent punishing the child, often the child is doing something that will harm them. The child might think freedom is doing that very thing, but the parent is protecting them because the parent knows what's best.

It's the same thing with God the Father; He knows what's best for His children. Even though His commandments might seem enslaving, He's actually giving us greater freedom.

THE FREEDOM TO WORK

Our sinful hearts confuse us in so many ways, and one of those ways is how blinded we are in our understanding of obedience. You see, sinful people think freedom is doing whatever we want. But like the child discussed above, that sort of boundless living will destroy us.

The freedom Jesus Christ purchased for us does not free us *from* obedience but frees us *to* obey. Once Jesus claims you as His, you will want to do what you ought to do. That is, the only kind of true Christian freedom that exists is the freedom to be and do what God created and redeemed us to be and do.

Therefore, Christian freedom is not freedom from obedience, but freedom to and for it. Any other thing that claims to be freedom is a wolf in sheep's clothing. Freedom to sin is, in fact, bondage.

Sadly, there are many teenagers who get caught up in the world of drugs. There are a variety of reasons for a pre-teen or teen to get into this world, but many times the idea of freedom is wrapped up in there. Maybe they thought they could make some extra cash and pursue a life that allowed them to have what they thought would be unattainable? Maybe they had relational issues with parents or friends, so they used this world as an escape? Whatever the case, they thought this lifestyle would buy them freedom, but they ended up purchasing their own slavery.

To be sure, this freedom does not mean you will never struggle against sin. The power of sin has been broken by Jesus, but its presence remains in us and around us. Obeying will be a life-long struggle, but the obedience we're called to pursue, by the grace of God, offers freedom.

THE HOPE OF SANCTIFICATION

For the Christian, fighting against sin can often feed thoughts of hopelessness. We can often feel like we'll never be able to grow in grace. We can look at our lives and wonder if we're even really a Christian at all. As we'll discuss later, there are sins we may wrestle with for the rest of our lives, but we must see the hope attached to our sanctification.

In sanctification we are set free from the bondage of sin's reign in our hearts. This does not set us free to a hopeless passivity towards our sin but to a hopeful activity. This is important to understand. So often, the Christian can look at a specific sin and think, *What's the point in praying about this sin, asking for God's strength? I give up. I cannot beat this.*

This is when we look to the Word of God through the apostle Paul for our strength, '[W]ork out your own salvation with fear and trembling, for it is God who works in you, both to will and work for his good pleasure' (Phil. 2:12b-13).

You see, our sanctification is not up to our effort and power. In many ways, our sanctification is God graciously showing us how weak we are and how badly we need Him. Sanctification is calling out to God saying, *God, I cannot win this battle over sin. God, I have no power to fight this. I need you to help me hate this sin. Give me strength.*

The hope of sanctification is constantly relying on grace. It is asking God for the grace to believe that your sin is already paid for by Christ. It is asking God for grace to give you hope that, '[H]e who began a good work in you will bring it to completion at the day of Jesus Christ' (Phil. 1:6). God is carrying us through the battle with our sin, and that must be our constant hope.

Main Point

God's forgiveness frees us to work for Him.

4. The God of Sanctification

There are many studies and stats that tell us many teenagers turn away from the church during college or post-college. Pastors and families are right to grieve over this. *What did we do wrong? Where did we fail?* These are understandable questions that haunt those who've experienced children leaving the church and, ultimately, leaving the faith.

Theologically speaking, we would say that any Christians who abandon the faith were never Christians to begin with. When God tells us that no one can snatch His children out of His hand (see John 10:27-30), that includes ourselves and our doubts.

People will assert numerous ways in which churches and parents failed in the discipleship of the next generation. While there is no foolproof system or mode we can implement into our church and home to prevent teens from turning away, one truth we must be sure to teach and speak about is suffering.

The Bible trains us to expect hardship and suffering as a part of Christianity. In the past, suffering and Christianity went hand-in-hand. Today, however, suffering can seem foreign to many Christians because we've been blessed with so much. Therefore, when students in the church have not been taught to expect suffering – of all kinds – they can quickly turn away, thinking that the Christian life isn't what they signed up for.

Suffering is an aspect of Christianity. It can take a variety of forms. One of those forms is the suffering we endure when fighting against our sin. The words *fight* and *warfare* are not hyperbole in the Christian life. The fight against our sinful flesh is as real as it gets, and that warfare is filled with pain and suffering. Sanctification is suffering.

GOD'S GOAL IN SANCTIFICATION

Even though the pain, suffering, and warfare of the Christian life seem daunting, it is important for us to keep this in mind. It gives us an important perspective and accurate expectations for our day-to-day living. This is a vital truth for teenagers today. As a Christian, you will suffer in your fight against sin.

But the glorious truth of sanctification means God will never give up on us and our growth. Even when we feel like giving up on ourselves and the church and our battle against sin, God doesn't give up. He doesn't get weary. He does not get tired of forgiving you for the 'same old sins.' He has made a promise, and He will carry you through the sufferings of this life.

In the last chapter, we talked about Philippians 1:6, and this must be a truth we celebrate. If you are a young Christian, you may have experienced discouragement in your sanctification. If you haven't, you will.

Satan will tempt you to despair. Your own sinful heart will lie to you and discourage you. Therefore, truths like God bringing His work to completion in us (see Phil. 1:6) are verses we must cling to and celebrate in the midst of our suffering. You may feel like giving up on the church, but God never feels like giving up on His children.

GOD'S GRACE IN SANCTIFICATION

So much of a Christian's sanctification is focused on work. It is true that there is work and effort and fighting involved in our sanctification. But the foundation of this work is the grace of God. All the fighting, all the praying, all the effort, points us to God's grace.

In fact, God's grace is just as powerfully demonstrated in our sanctification as in our justification. Our justification is that one-time work of Jesus Christ dying on the cross. His righteous life was credited to us, and our filthy sin was placed on Him, by faith – and that faith is a gift of God, so we cannot boast (see Eph. 2:8-9). It is all a work of God's grace.

This is the case for sanctification as well. No human would naturally see their sin, had God not graciously revealed it to them. Once revealed, no Christian has the faith to believe in Jesus without grace. Once saved, no Christian has the strength without the gracious work and power of the Spirit within them. Once the Spirit resides in the Christian, none of them would endure through the trials of life, without God's continual grace bestowed every second of every hour of every day.

Sanctification is a work of grace.

GOD'S GOODNESS IN SANCTIFICATION

It may be easy to see God's goodness in sanctification because we've just seen that He never gives up on us and He is graciously providing for us in this process. And those are good truths to be encouraged by, but there's more.

Sanctification is ultimately encouraging even when we are discouraged by ongoing sin. It can be encouraging even when we see a lack of progress. *Why?* You may ask. Because our sanctification is God's work.

Have you ever worked? I don't mean, 'do you have a job?' But have you worked in the yard or cleaned up your room? Any type of work. Whether you like it or not, whether you grumble and complain about doing work, there is a sense of accomplishment once finished. I, for one, take great pleasure in seeing my yard after I mow it – I love seeing my work.

In a much deeper way, you and I need to see that 'We are [God's] workmanship, created in Christ Jesus for good works…' (Eph. 2:10). God looks at His children and smiles. He sees you and me as His work, and He takes pleasure in that.

God never gives up working in us, God graciously strengthens and moves us along in this life, and God's goodness can be seen through His work in our life.

Main Point

God never gives up on our sanctification.

5. The Fullness of Sanctification

GOD'S IMAGE BREAKERS

One of the most fundamental biblical truths is that all of humanity has been created in God's image. At the dawn of creation, God created humans to bear His image throughout His creation. Humans were set apart from all of creation, because of this unique truth. However, mankind sinned against this good Creator and tarnished that image. Yes, humanity still bears the image of God, but this image is now flawed.

In sanctification we realize that God is fixing that. Sanctification is God fully restoring His image in you. That is why Paul prays 'that you may be filled with all the fullness of God' (Eph. 3:19). Because we still bear God's image in us, we know something is wrong with us.

All of humanity has a longing for restoration deep inside them. You'll hear it in songs, you'll see it in movies, you'll read it in other stories –

there is a desire to be restored to our original state of perfection. Through sanctification, God is restoring that image in each of us. This will not be fully realized until we are in heaven with God, but sanctification is allowing us to die more to sin and live more to righteousness.

THE SON'S IMAGE

Theology can be dangerous; did you know that? Let me explain.

At its most basic level, theology is the study of God. Any time we study God or seek to understand God, we also risk misunderstanding Him or misinterpreting His Word. Since we are all sinners and our hearts are poisoned with sin, the way we talk about theology can be flawed.

Similarly, a discussion about sanctification is risky. It can make us uncomfortable because we talk about work in the Christian life. We talk about growing in godliness. We talk about becoming more holy. To some, this can sound like a misunderstanding of God's work in salvation and what it means to be saved by grace through faith – theology can be dangerous.

We just talked about humanity being created in God's image, but that image is now flawed because of sin. Although it is flawed, God is working through sanctification to restore His image. And this would not be possible without the finished work of Jesus Christ.

Sanctification is how God makes us to be like Jesus. As the apostle Paul says, [God's children] will be 'conformed to the image of his Son' (Rom. 8:29). God is restoring His image in His children because His Son lived the perfect life and died the perfect death. Jesus secured this restored image for God's children.

IT'S NOT MY FAULT

Have you ever noticed how quickly we want to blame others for things that are truly our fault? If you get angry at someone, you blame them for being annoying instead of seeing how your own sin made you react the way you did. Perhaps you accuse someone else of gossip; however, when you really stop and think about it, you asked them questions with the hopes of leading the conversation down that path. We need humility to see our faults more often.

Not only do we often recoil at admitting fault, we also trumpet our good deeds as if they were really ours. Sanctification gives us a humble heart and mind to see the evils of our heart, but it also gives us humility to see that the good we do is only because of grace.

Augustine once prayed, 'O Lord, everything good in me is due to you. The rest is my fault.' Yes, this can sting our pride a bit, but that's a good thing.

It is good to trumpet God's name and not our own. It's good to admit that we are sinful and often more at fault than we realize. It's also good to have eyes and ears to hear and see God's gracious good deeds that He works through us. It's good to have this perspective on the Christian life, and it's all because of God's work through sanctification.

As God conforms us more into the image of His Son through the sanctification process, we can sincerely echo the words of the psalmist, 'Not to us, O LORD, not to us, but to your name give glory, for the sake of your steadfast love and your faithfulness!' (Ps. 115:1).

Main Point

Through sanctification, God is restoring His fallen creation.

6. Do This! Don't Do That!

Encouragement is one of those words we use a lot, but we sometimes lessen its meaning. Many of us hear the word 'encouragement' and we think in terms of kind words or words of affirmation. 'You're a great person.' 'I really like your personality.' 'You're such a thoughtful friend.' These, I would guess, are statements many would file away in the encouragement section.

While these are properly labeled, there might be some words of encouragement that seem a little less positive. Even the specific word can be used in a stronger context. 'Let me encourage you to rethink your position on the matter.' 'I would encourage you to stop using that phrase around me.'

In other words, encouragement could be used to speak words of challenge to others. Confrontational words to those who might not want to hear them. The word 'courage' is there as a root, after all.

If you consider the word more, you'll discover that words associated with 'encourage' are words like: stir, press, challenge, fire up, pressure, push, etc. These can all have positive and negative connotations. If nothing else, they should deepen our understanding of 'encouragement.' It's not just a word that passes along light-hearted, self-esteem-building phrases.

If one looks at the words of Christ in the New Testament, there are many encouraging words He speaks. He tells us to 'love one another' (John 13:34). At face value that sounds like a very positive statement. However, have you ever realized how hard it is to love someone else? I don't know about you, but I like myself a lot. And I can often find it hard to love others more than myself. Therefore, Christ's command to love one another can actually be a discouraging (not encouraging) command – unless we think about it in light of sanctification.

You see, sanctification is what God does in us so we can obey Jesus' new commandment in the book of John. Sanctification is how we are able to 'love one another: just as I [Jesus] have loved you' (13:34). By God's work in us, we can at least make a start at obeying that colossal 'encouragement.'

Once we really stop and think about what Jesus is encouraging us to do by this command – and many others, for that matter – we feel the weight of it. Rather than being crushed under its weight, however, we can be encouraged that sanctification is why Jesus can command us to do these things. It forces us to deal with the ugliness of our hearts and call upon the Spirit for strength. True encouragement is being challenged and drawn into deeper communion with Christ.

STOPPING AND STARTING

When I first learned how to ride a bike, I can remember that the stopping and starting were the biggest challenges. Now that the training wheels were off, I had to maintain balance when I started and stopped. Once I got going, my momentum would carry me pretty easily.

The Christian life can sometimes feel like riding a bike. Maybe we're trying to stop a certain sin pattern or start a biblical command in our life. It can seem downright impossible sometimes. We can easily despair over certain things. Truth be told, it's all impossible for us on our own. Even the desire to start, or stop, was initiated by God's Spirit, and it's His power that carries us through.

As we're talking about Christ's encouraging words to live in certain ways, we have to consider many of the imperatives in the New Testament. Imperatives are those verses we come across that command us to 'do this' or 'don't do that.' They are often read as commands or rules for the Christian life. Yes, the Bible is more than a book of rules, but it does contain those rules of encouragement... there's that word again.

Sanctification is how Christians can respond to these imperatives properly. As one begins to read through the New Testament, there are hundreds of imperatives. If someone does not understand the biblical truth of sanctification, they will misunderstand the imperatives. In fact, if they misunderstand sanctification, they will live as a legalist. They will try to start or stop in their own strength – not relying on the strength of the Spirit.

Sanctification is not afraid to talk about the imperatives in the Bible. Sanctification sees the commands through the gracious lens of God's work in us. It makes sense of how God could expect His children to live a certain way, even when our hearts desire to live another way.

The good news of sanctification is that it is a divine grace-work. It is designed to give us hope, not discouragement. John Newton understood this. Newton said: 'I am not what I ought to be, I am not what I want to be, I am not what I hope to be... but still I am not what I once used to be, and by the grace of God I am what I am.'

Newton knew that there were things he wanted to stop doing and things he wanted to start doing, but he was also aware that God's grace had carried him away from what he once was. Sanctification is the gracious hope to live the Christian life in the way God *encourages* us to.

Main Point

God's commands call us to action, not passiveness.

7. Trust and Obey

There's an old movie where two moronic criminals burst into a bank lobby to perform the clichéd robbery. As they rush into the bank with shotguns in hand, one of them screams, 'Everybody freeze! Everybody down on the ground!' After a lengthy pause, an old man in the bank lobby replies, 'Well, which is it, young feller? You want I should freeze or get down on the ground? Mean to say, if'n I freeze, I can't rightly drop. And if'n I drop, I'm a-gonna be in motion.'

There's a sense in which sanctification feels the same way. Are we to work as Christians or are we to rest as Christians? Are we to freeze (not do anything) or are we to drop to the ground (do something)? The answer? Yes.

The truth of sanctification shows how God's sovereignty and our responsibility work together in the Christian life. God's sovereignty is a theological word that gives Christians an image of a King. You can see the word *reign* in the word *sovereign*. God is enthroned, and He is ruling and reigning over all of creation.

To be sure, humanity cannot fully comprehend God's omnipotent (all-powerful) and omniscient (all-knowing) reign. Our tiny minds cannot fully understand this truth, but we grasp that God is in control of everything that happens in the lives of humanity.

Therefore, nothing happens on God's earth without God's control and approval.

At the same time, God also commands His children to live and act in a specific way (we discussed this in the previous chapter). He gives them responsibility to live in a way that He expects Christians to live. To love God and love others, sums up the life of the Christian. This is how God calls His children to live.

But if you've lived on this earth for any length of time, you realize that your sinful heart doesn't want to love God and love others above yourself. We love ourselves so much.

Well, which is it? Is God sovereign or is mankind responsible to live a certain way? Yes.

LET'S GO FOR A BIKE RIDE

One of the most helpful illustrations I've heard on God's sovereignty came from Rankin Wilbourne's book, *Union with Christ*. I do not think the illustration is original to him, but it's helpful.

Picture a bike. While there are many different makes and models, all bikes have two tires and two pedals. The front tire represents God's grace. His work, His love, His mercy, His sovereignty – you absolutely need that front tire to ride the bike. In the Christian life, you absolutely need God's grace to survive one second on this earth.

The back tire represents God's commands (or imperatives, from the last chapter). God commands His children to live a certain way. When riding a bike, you absolutely need that back tire as well. God's commands are for His glory and our good. When we live in the manner He calls us to, it reflects His character throughout the world – this should point all of humanity to Him.

You need those two tires, but you also need two pedals. The pedals represent faith and repentance. Faith and repentance mark the beginning of the Christian life. That is, once we first become a Christian, we place our faith in the finished work of Jesus, and we repent of our sins.

That said, we also repent and believe for the remainder of our lives on earth. We never move past faith and repentance. We must, by God's grace, continually place our faith in what Jesus has done, and repent of the sins we commit daily.

Just like you cannot ride a bike without pedals, you cannot live the Christian life without faith and repentance. Therefore, by God's grace, the Christian is to press down on faith and press down on repentance (like pedaling a bike) each day of their life.

In summary, the front tire is grace, the back tire is work, and the two pedals that you continue to press on are faith and repentance. And, as we have said, the only reason we can press down on the pedals of faith and repentance is the work of God's Spirit. The Holy Spirit worked in our hearts to make us repent and believe, and He continues to give us the strength to do that in this life.

In many ways, the work of the Christian life and the resting in Christ's finished work is easy to grasp. Yet, it is also baffling. How much do we work and how much do we rest? Pointing us back to Philippians 2:12-13, 'Therefore, my beloved, as you have always obeyed, so now, not only as in my presence but much more in my absence, work out your own salvation with fear and trembling, for it is God who works in you, both to will and to work for his good pleasure.' Paul tells the believers in Philippi to *work* and *obey*, knowing that it's God working in them – this isn't a contradiction.

Not only is the truth of God's sovereignty and humanity's responsibility a theological truth, it's also a joy. This truth is meant to move us to joy. This is why we can sing the words of the old hymn, 'Trust and obey, for there's no other way, to be happy in Jesus, but to trust and obey.' To be happy in the finished work of Jesus, we trust His work and we seek, by His grace, to obey. This is all for God's glory and our good.

Main Point

Keep trusting. Keep obeying.

8. A Long Time Ago, In a Galaxy Far, Far Away

Becoming a father is one of the greatest joys in life. It's also extremely humbling. Being a parent definitely brings you to the end of yourself. You quickly realize how much you don't know, and are confronted with your sin in many ways.

One of the challenges I was confronted with came about through my children's questions. If you aren't a parent, just know that kids ask questions… all… the… time. *What's that? What's her name? How did you do that? Are we there yet? Why?* To be honest, the constant peppering of questions can start to work on your sanctification. In other words, it can be a little annoying.

However, there was an aspect of my children's inquiries that really humbled me. And that is this: *It can be really hard to explain some things.* It can be hard to explain the simplest, every-day experiences of life – Dad, why do they call these shoes? Dad, why is the grass green? Dad, why are carrots shaped that way? Dad, how come that man honked his horn at you? Dad, what does it mean to be frustrated?

On the other end of the spectrum are questions that deal with the complexities of life in a fallen world – Dad, what does abortion mean? Dad, how can a man become a woman? Dad, my friend's daddy doesn't live with them anymore, why?

The questions I receive from my children expose my lack of intellect, my inability to communicate in an understanding manner, and my impatience when I dismiss their questions because I don't feel like answering them.

One thing is for sure, I have learned how patient my heavenly Father is with me. I have realized how gracious He is to answer so many of life's questions in His Word. I have learned how He doesn't dismiss me – ever – when I need to talk to Him in prayer. I have realized that He is the best Father a child could have.

And, while all of that is true, there are answers to my questions that I just don't understand.

There are times, when I ponder some of life's questions, and I realize how small I am. I may ask a question, and then I'm confronted by my finiteness and God's infinite wisdom and glory.

For example, I believe in the biblical doctrine of the Trinity, but there's a point when my mind cannot comprehend it. It is a truth I can believe, I can understand – to an extent, I can see it in the Bible, but it's a mystery that's beyond my tiny, little mind.

Sanctification is that way as well.

SANCTIFICATION IS BIGGER THAN YOU THINK

We're beginning to wrap up this little book on sanctification. I hope your understanding of sanctification has been challenged and strengthened. I hope you realize how much of your life is wrapped up in this doctrine, and I hope your knowledge of Jesus has grown from the truths mentioned. Still, while there's much we can understand about sanctification, there's much that will remain a mystery to us.

Want to think about something that might make your brain hurt? Not literally but it may challenge your mental capacity a bit. Consider this: One of the mysteries of sanctification is that our own sanctification existed before we did. Our own sanctification was around prior to us even being born. Confused? Think with me a second.

The good news of sanctification should remind us of the astonishing truth that God has always had it in His mind. It wasn't 'plan B' for God, because He doesn't have a 'plan B.' God has always been in existence, and He is all-knowing (omniscient). Therefore, He has always known about our sanctification.

Since God has always been around, He was working on our sanctification from eternity past, long before creation, before we existed. If you need to take Tylenol and sit down a minute, that's fine. Now, this isn't just some crazy notion that popped into my head one day. Or an interesting thought that some brilliant theologian invented. God tells us this in His Word.

Paul says we were created for 'good works, which God prepared beforehand, that we should walk in them' (Eph. 2:10). God created us for good works that were prepared beforehand. Are we robots? No. Does God know what we're going to do? Yes.

To put it provocatively, trillions of years ago, God was already preparing your progress in sanctification in the Christian life. That's crazy! And, like we said earlier, that's a truth we can read from the Bible and grasp to an extent, but we cannot fully understand. Even though it's something we cannot understand, it's still good news… amazing is more accurate.

Hopefully that helps you see how vast this doctrine is. Hopefully this truth from this verse encourages you. A good God, who is omniscient and omnipotent, prepared good works for you to walk in before your life even began.

Now that's a loving Father.

Main Point

Our sanctification is a display of God's goodness and love.

Conclusion: Working For Your New Master

We began this short book discussing how sanctification is a word that's often viewed in a negative light. It's a theological truth that's often seen as discouraging. Not only is it seen as negative or discouraging, it can lead to error that impacts the Christian life in a variety of ways. This error could be manifested in misery and guilt for the Christian, or, to a further extent – false teaching.

There are some who hear the word 'sanctification' and think that Christian faith is our work. It's something that requires our effort to keep us in good standing with God. As we've seen, the Christian life does require effort, but it's fueled by the inner working of God's Spirit. As we said, we are to work, but it is God working in us (see Phil. 2:12-13).

There are others who hear 'sanctification' but they are so afraid of sounding legalistic that they tend to downplay the work of a Christian. Since Jesus did all the work required to save the believer, any talk about work makes them uncomfortable. In a noble effort to emphasize Christ's work, these Christians excuse others from feeling the need to strive towards godliness.

While there's no perfect story or illustration that fully encompasses this doctrine, and, as we mentioned in the previous chapter, there will always be some mystery to sanctification, I think this story from Sally Lloyd-Jones gets at the heart of the doctrine:

There is a story from the American Civil War of a Northerner who bought a young slave girl at a slave auction. As they left the auction, the man turned to the girl and said, 'You're free!' She turned to him in amazement, 'You mean I'm free to do whatever I want?' 'Yes,' he said.

'And to say whatever I want to say?' 'Yes, anything.' 'And to be whatever I want to be?' 'Yes!'

'And even go wherever I want to go?' 'Yes!' He laughed. 'You're free to go wherever you'd like!'

She looked at him intently and replied, 'Then I will go with you.'[1]

This is a beautiful story that helps us get to the heart of this doctrine. You see, God's children were once enslaved to sin. We were running from God. We were not seeking Him. We were living in our sin, and our sin was destroying us.

God, however, comes along and purchases us through the life and death of His Son. He buys us through the righteous blood of Christ. He adopts us into His family and promises to carry us home through the strength of the Spirit.

Through this act of salvation, God gives us freedom from our sin. Even though we still have sin in our heart and we – at times – long for our sin and think that God's ways don't give us freedom, true freedom is only found in Him.

Just like the slave girl, Christians realize their new Master is a gracious one. This Master does not require the back-breaking labor our sin required. This new Master does not place the heavy burden of the law on us because He placed it on Another in order to save us.

---

1   Lloyd-Jones, Sally, *Thoughts to Make Your Heart Sing* (Zonderkidz: 2012), 118.

The slave girl wants to walk with this Master. The slave girl wants to work for this Master. The slave girl wants to be in the presence of this Master.

You see, she realizes the former life she had was not a life of freedom. Yes, the new life she has requires work, but it was by the work of Another that she has this new life. The work in this new life is a work of joy. She realizes that she did not have to work to be purchased and accepted. She was purchased first and works for this gracious Master from this mindset.

What about you? Is this your Master? Do you see the Christian life as a life of true freedom? Do you see that sanctification really is a gracious and encouraging truth?

There are true Christians who have been Christians for years and years but miss this encouragement. They miss the freedom that's in the work God requires of His children. They miss the joy.

There are also those who aren't Christians. Perhaps that's you? Maybe you think the Christian life is joyless? Maybe you think it's up to you to work your way into God's favor and Kingdom? If that's you, I hope you see the gracious nature of God and the work Jesus did to bring people into the Kingdom. It's not up to your work. It's not up to your effort.

Rest in the work of Jesus, so you can work alongside Him in this life… and the life to come.

Appendix A: What Now?

- Stop and analyze your own heart. Do you truly believe in Jesus Christ? Have you repented of your sin and placed your faith in His finished work?

- Thank God for being so gracious and faithful as to make you His child.

- Reflect upon the wickedness of your sin and what Jesus did to pay for it.

- Reflect upon the reality that you are truly righteous because of what Jesus did.

- Are you living under constant guilt? Is it because you're trying to earn your own righteousness before God?

- What sins have you become too comfortable with in your life? Ask God to help you see your sins and give you the strength to fight against them.

- Do you have any sort of devotional life? Are you spending time in God's Word or prayer? Ask God for strength to pursue this.

- Talk to your parents or pastors about their own struggles in Christianity. Ask them what God taught them from these struggles. Ask them for advice on struggles of your own.

- Think of older Christians you respect in your own church. Why do you respect them? While they are sinners as well, what are some godly qualities you see in them? Maybe you can strive towards some of those patterns by God's grace and strength?

Often times sanctification can be a discouraging truth, but we must be reminded that God promises to bring this work to completion in His children.

Appendix B: Other Books on this Topic

Jerry Bridges, *Respectable Sins, Student Edition: The Truth about Anger, Jealousy, Worry, and Other Stuff We Accept* (TH1NK, 2014).

Jerry Bridges, *The Chase: Pursuing Holiness in Your Everyday Life* (NavPress, 2003).

Jerry Bridges, *The Pursuit of Holiness* (NavPress, 1978).

Tim Chester, *You Can Change: God's Transforming Power for Our Sinful Behavior and Negative Emotions* (IVP, 2008).

Kevin DeYoung, *The Hole in Our Holiness: Filling the Gap Between Gospel Passion and the Pursuit of Godliness* (Crossway, 2014).

J.V. Fesko, *A Christian's Pocket Guide to Growing in Holiness* (Christian Focus Publications, 2012).

Kris Lundgaard, *The Enemy Within: Straight Talk about the Power and Defeat of Sin* (P&R, 1998).

J.C. Ryle, *Holiness: Its Nature, Hindrances, Difficulties, and Roots* (Banner of Truth, 2014).

R.C. Sproul, *The Holiness of God* (Tyndale, 1985).

Glossary

Antinomian – Someone who doesn't live by God's law; a person who lives however they want to live. In many ways this person would be the opposite of a legalist.

God the Father – God is one Being and three Persons; referred to as the Trinity. The Father, the Son, & the Holy Spirit make up the three Persons of the One God. Each Person is eternal and equal in essence. God the Father is the Creator of all things and rules over everything. God, in His grace, promised to save His sinful children from their rebellion. He adopts His children through the finished work of His Son, Jesus.

Godliness – Living in a manner that reflects the character of God. While no human can reach perfection in this life, striving by the Spirit to live in a godly way is the fruit of being a Christian (see also 'Holy').

Grace – The undeserved favor and goodness of God poured out on His enemies. When God makes you His child, it is because of His grace alone. Grace is not something you can earn.

Holy Spirit – God is one Being and three Persons; referred to as the Trinity. The Father, the Son, & the Holy Spirit make up the three Persons of the One God. Each Person is eternal and equal in essence. The Holy Spirit is often referred to as the strength of the Christian. The Spirit is given to all believers and helps us live every aspect of the Christian life.

Holy/Holiness – Set apart, different. God is infinitely and eternally 'other' and completely set apart from all beings. When Christians strive by grace to live holy lives, they will be set apart and different from the world.

Imperative – A command. In the Bible, we read of many commands from God. These imperatives, or commands, are to be read in light of Jesus' finished work. Some people can think that God's imperative statements are harsh, but they are gracious. He is telling us how we can best live in a way that brings Him glory and brings about good in the life of His people. These imperative statements are to be pursued by the power of the Spirit, with the knowledge that Jesus lived perfectly for us.

In Christ – A Christian is completely united to Christ. The phrase 'in Christ' is repeated throughout the Bible and this refers to our union with Him. We are completely secure as God's children and no one can take that away.

Jesus Christ – God is one Being and three Persons; referred to as the Trinity. The Father, the Son, & the Holy Spirit make up the three Persons of the One God. Each Person is eternal and equal in essence. Jesus Christ is God's eternal Son. Jesus Christ is fully God and has always been in existence. He appears at times in the Old Testament, but He added flesh to His deity when He was born of a virgin birth by the Holy Spirit. He lived a perfect life and died a death on the cross for God's children. He is the only Savior of sinners.

Justification – The one-time act where God declared His children righteous, by the finished work of His Son Jesus. Jesus lived a fully righteous life and gives that righteousness to His Father's children, by faith. Jesus also took the sins of God's children on Himself when

He died on the cross. That one-time act – 'It is finished' – justified God's children.

Law – In a general sense, this refers to God's perfect design and way of life for His creation. Since sin has entered the world, God's people cannot perfectly keep His law and are therefore declared guilty. Since God is a perfectly just judge and His law reveals His good character, He sent Jesus to perfectly obey the law for His children.

Legalist – Someone who tries to obey God's Word perfectly in their own strength. They think they can earn God's favor on their own, by working hard to keep the law; which is impossible. This would be the opposite of an antinomian; see also 'works righteousness'.

Positional sanctification – (Note: Some people separate sanctification into two categories) This refers to the reality that all Christians are fully and completely sanctified, because of Jesus' finished work. Since true Christians are 'in Christ' and justified before God the Father, there is a sense in which they are positionally holy and sanctified right now.

Progressive sanctification – (Note: Some people separate sanctification into two categories). This refers to the ongoing work of the Christian to 'progress in their holiness' by God's grace. Even though true Christians become more aware of their sin and brokenness as they grow older, there is a sense in which they become more sanctified; i.e., progress. (See 1 Corinthians 6:11; Paul talks of our sanctification in past tense.)

Redemption – God's work of perfecting His sinful children through the work of the Spirit and Jesus.

Repentance – An act of God's grace that moves sinners to turn from their sin and turn to Jesus. In order to be a Christian, we must repent of our sin and place our faith in Jesus. That said, repentance is a continual practice of Christians since we battle with sin until we go to heaven.

Sanctification – This is the essence of the Christian life. This is the ongoing work of Christians fighting against sin and living in a righteous/holy/godly way. Christians cannot work in their own strength; they can only work by the power of the Holy Spirit.

Sin – It is anti-God; sin is completely opposed to all that is good and is so horrible, it took the death of God's Son to save us. It is thinking, saying, or doing anything that God forbids in the Bible. It can also refer to disobeying God's commands. Sin brings every form of pain, suffering, & sadness into God's creation.

Sovereignty – God's complete rule and reign over all creation. Kings can also be referred to as Sovereigns, so this term points to God's Kingly rule over everyone and everything.

Temptation – Our sinful heart's desire to think, say, or do things that go against God's teaching in the Bible. It also refers to spiritual warfare. Even though are hearts are poisoned with sin, Satan and his demons are also at work to make us live in a way that opposes God's Word.

Theology – The study of God; vital to the life of a Christian. To love Jesus well, Christians must strive to have a solid theology from the Bible.

Word (of God) – The Bible or Scriptures. Since God wrote the entire Bible through humans, we call it God's Word.

Works (Righteousness) – refers to a practice where people try to earn God's favor. When people believe they can work their way to heaven by their own 'good' works. This goes against the teaching of the Bible. Jesus was the only righteous one and He gives us His righteous works by faith. See also 'legalist'.

Watch out for other forthcoming books in the
Track series, including:

Sanctification
Technology
Prayer
Body Image
Music
Rest
Addiction
Marketing

Reformed Youth Ministries (RYM) exists to reach students for Christ and equip them to serve. Passing the faith on to the next generation has been RYM's passion since it began. In 1972 three youth workers who shared a passion for biblical teaching to youth surveyed the landscape of youth ministry conferences. What they found was an emphasis on fun and games, not God's Word. Therefore, they started a conference that focused on the preaching and teaching of God's Word. Over the years RYM has grown beyond conferences into three areas of ministry: conferences, training, and resources.

- **Conferences:** RYM's youth conferences take place in the summer at a variety of locations across the United States and are continuing to expand. We also host parenting conferences throughout the year at local churches.

- **Training:** RYM launched an annual Youth Leader Training (YLT) conference in 2008. YLT has grown steadily through the years and is offered in multiple locations. RYM also offers a Church Internship Program in partnering local churches as well as youth leader coaching and youth ministry consulting.
- **Resources:** RYM offers a variety of resources for leaders, parents, and students. Several Bible studies are offered as free downloads with more titles regularly being added to their catalogue. RYM hosts multiple podcasts: *Parenting Today*, *The Local Youth Worker*, & *The RYM Student Podcast* – all of which can be downloaded on multiple formats. There are many additional ministry tools available for download on the website.

If you are passionate for passing the faith on to the next generation, please visit www.rym.org to learn more about Reformed Youth Ministries. If you are interested in partnering with us in ministry, please visit www.rym.org/donate.

Christian Focus Publications

Our mission statement —

STAYING FAITHFUL

In dependence upon God we seek to impact the world through literature faithful to His infallible Word, the Bible. Our aim is to ensure that the Lord Jesus Christ is presented as the only hope to obtain forgiveness of sin, live a useful life and look forward to heaven with Him.

Our books are published in four imprints:

CHRISTIAN
FOCUS

Popular works including biographies, commentaries, basic doctrine and Christian living.

CHRISTIAN
HERITAGE

Books representing some of the best material from the rich heritage of the church.

MENTOR

Books written at a level suitable for Bible College and seminary students, pastors, and other serious readers. The imprint includes commentaries, doctrinal studies, examination of current issues and church history.

CF4•K

Children's books for quality Bible teaching and for all age groups: Sunday school curriculum, puzzle and activity books; personal and family devotional titles, biographies and inspirational stories — because you are never too young to know Jesus!

Christian Focus Publications Ltd,
Geanies House, Fearn, Ross-shire,
IV20 1TW, Scotland, United Kingdom.
www.christianfocus.com
blog.christianfocus.com